Rose Elliot's Book o~ ~~~

Rose Elliot is the author of several bestselling
cookbooks, and is renowned for her practical
and creative approach. She writes regularly for
the *Vegetarian* and has contributed to national
newspapers and magazines as well as broad-
casting on radio and television. She is married
and has three children.

Rose Elliot's Book of

Salads

Fontana Paperbacks

First published by Fontana Paperbacks 1983

Set in 10 on 11pt Linotron Plantin
Illustrations by Vana Haggerty
Made and printed in Great Britain by
William Collins Sons & Co. Ltd, Glasgow

Introduction

Salads are quick, cheap and fun to make: of all the branches of cookery, salad-making can be one of the pleasantest and most rewarding. A mixed salad allows great scope for combining colours and textures and for arranging them attractively on the plate, while a simple salad, speedily made from crisp, fresh ingredients, is often the perfect accompaniment to a cooked meal.

So salad-making is a skill worth mastering and it's not at all difficult.

EQUIPMENT

The equipment needed for salad-making is simple and basic: a wooden serving bowl and servers, a salad spinner for drying leafy vegetables, a large chopping board and a sharp knife. An electric grater saves time if you're going to make many salads which require chopping and grating. I like an autochop for chopping cabbage and root vegetables; it is quick and produces the right sort of texture. A blender is useful for making mayonnaise and some dressings, though not essential.

A wide variety of vegetables and fruits can be used in salads, together with ingredients such as rice, pulses, pasta and dairy produce. Here are some suggestions.

Avocado pear Should feel slightly soft all over when cradled in the palm of your hand. Cut in half using a stainless steel knife, remove stone and skin, then slice or dice. Sprinkle with lemon juice to preserve colour.

Beansprouts Mung bean sprouts and alfalfa sprouts bring a crunchy texture to salads; wash, drain and add to salad mixtures.

Beetroot Can be used both cooked and raw. Slip the skins off cooked beetroot and slice or dice; peel and grate raw beetroot. In either case serve on its own in an oil and vinegar, honey and cider vinegar or soured cream dressing. Grated raw beetroot is pleasant mixed with grated apple and raisins and dressed with orange juice.

Brussels sprouts Use small firm ones; wash, trim and chop or slice and add to mixed salads.

Cabbage Choose crisp pale green varieties, also white 'salad cabbage' and red cabbage. Cut into quarters, wash and trim; remove central core. Shred fairly finely; mix with a tasty dressing. Cabbage makes a good base for other more colourful ingredients: see page 23.

Carrots Scrub or scrape. Grate finely or coarsely as desired, or cut into fingers for serving with dips. Cover quickly with vinaigrette or orange or lemon juice to prevent discoloration.

Cauliflower Wash, trim and cut into florets. Chop or grate and mix with a creamy dressing, or cook lightly then toss in vinaigrette.

Celeriac Peel, then grate or cut into matchsticks. Good with a peppery vinaigrette or a creamy dressing.

Celery Wash, removing outer stalks and leaves, then slice, dice or serve in sticks.

Chicory Trim and wash, removing any damaged leaves. Slice into rings, cut down into quarters or eighths or just separate the leaves.

Chinese cabbage, Chinese leaves Wash, trim and shred. Useful for quick salads, especially in winter.

Cucumber Wash cucumber; leave skin on, peel or remove strips of skin, then slice, dice or coarsely grate. Mix with lemon juice and seasonings, or with natural yoghurt or soured cream, for a refreshing salad.

Dried fruit Raisins, sultanas, chopped dried apricots and dates add a delicious touch of sweetness to a salad, especially one made from cabbage or root vegetables.

Endive, escarole and batavia Separate and wash the leaves, discarding outer ones; tear inner ones into pieces.

Fennel Trim off root and any tough leaves, then wash and slice. Particularly good mixed with grated carrot, apple and cucumber or with cubed cooked beetroot and walnuts.

French beans Should be small, firm and crisp. A few chopped raw beans can be added to a mixed salad, but they are particularly delicious when first lightly cooked, as in salade Niçoise (page 49).

7

Fruit Fresh fruit, prepared and cut as necessary, can be delicious in mixed salads, adding just the right contrast in texture, colour and flavour. Try apples with cabbage, celery, fennel and root vegetables; pineapple and cabbage; oranges with watercress, onions and carrots. Bananas, peaches, pears, grapes and strawberries can also be included.

Lamb's lettuce, corn salad A good winter salad ingredient to grow: treat as lettuce.

Leeks Thinly slice tender leeks and add to salads for a subtle onion flavour; or cook leeks whole, drain and cover with vinaigrette.

Lettuce Trim off stems and coarse leaves; wash in cold water and shake dry. Put into a polythene bag and keep in the fridge for an hour or so, if possible, to crisp up.

Mushrooms Wash, trim and thinly slice small white button mushrooms; mix with vinaigrette and leave for 1-2 hours before serving. Or cook in olive oil then cool: (page 37).

Nuts Chop and add to salad mixtures for extra texture and flavour as well as protein. Walnuts, hazel nuts, cashews and brazils are all suitable, also roasted peanuts and desiccated coconut.

Olives Make a delicious, piquant addition to a salad. Buy plump, juicy, black olives loose at a delicatessen or choose a good canned or bottled brand.

Onions Remove skin, chop onions or cut into thin rounds. Make a pungent, crunchy addition to mixed salads.

Parsnips Peel, grate coarsely and mix with creamy dressings such as mayonnaise or yoghurt.

Pasta Cooked pasta makes a good basis for a substantial salad and absorbs flavours well. Cook as described on page 51.

Peppers Add colour and texture to mixed salads. Wash, de-seed and chop or slice.

Potatoes Cooked new or old potatoes make a delicious salad. Boil until just tender, drain, dice and mix with vinaigrette, mayonnaise or soured cream.

Pulses Dried beans and lentils make good salads on their own, with a well-flavoured dressing, or can be added to other salads for extra interest and nourishment. Many types are suitable, especially butter beans, red kidney beans, haricot beans, chick peas and whole lentils. See recipes on pages 42, 43, 48 and 49.

Radishes Wash and trim. If leafy tops are still attached and look fresh these can be left on if the radishes are being served as a nibble or with a dip. Peel then dice or grate winter radish.

Rice Cooked rice mixed with colourful ingredients makes an excellent salad; use long-grain brown rice and cook as described for moulded rice salad on page 54.

Salad cress Trim close to the roots; wash and drain in colander or sieve. Add to mixed salads or use as a garnish.

Sesame, sunflower and pumpkin seeds Add just before serving to give a crisp texture and increase the nutritional value of salads.

Spinach Wash and dry; shred and add to green or mixed salad.

Spring onions Trim off roots and some of the green tops; serve whole, in a mixed salad bowl or with dips; or chop and add.

Swedes Use in the same way as parsnips.

Sweetcorn Cooked sweetcorn makes a pleasant addition to a mixed salad, especially a rice or pasta salad and is also good with a spicy dressing (page 57).

Tomatoes Look for really firm tomatoes. Either leave the skin on or remove by covering the tomatoes with boiling water for 1 minute, then drain and slip off the skins with a sharp knife. Slice into rounds or cut in half and then into thin slivers. See recipe on page 58.

Turnips Use as for parsnips, but in small quantities as turnip is strongly flavoured.

Watercress or land cress Remove tough stalks and any damaged leaves. Wash and dry carefully. Serve on its own with a light dressing, use as a garnish or add to other salads. Watercress will keep for a day or two if put head-down in a bowl containing 6 mm (½in) water and stored in the fridge.

MAKING THE DRESSING

Most salad dressings are easy to make and if you use good ingredients you can't go wrong. To dress a salad simply I think it's quickest to mix all the ingredients in the salad bowl, pop the salad in on top then gently turn it with a pair of salad servers. However there are times when it's useful to have dressings made up separately and you will find recipes for these below.

For most salads nothing can beat the delicious fruity flavour of olive oil, though a light, flavourless oil such as sunflower is useful for some, particularly fruit mixtures, and for making mayonnaise. Sesame, walnut and hazel oil have a pronounced flavour which is pleasant for a change. It's also fun to experiment with different vinegars. I like red wine vinegar for most purposes, but fruity flavoured cider and raspberry vinegar make an interesting change and so does light-tasting rice vinegar.

You can also vary the basic dressing by adding herbs, spices and other flavourings: mustard, fresh herbs, crushed garlic, grated fresh ginger root, soy sauce, tomato purée or ketchup, crushed coriander seeds, paprika and curry powder are all good.

When it comes to creamy dressings, the ultimate luxury is undoubtedly a perfectly made mayonnaise. This can be mixed with natural yoghurt, soured cream or fromage blanc; these also make good dressings in their own right, as does curd cheese and tofu, a soft soya curd which you can buy at Chinese stores and health shops.

Here are some recipes for various kinds of salad dressings:

Simple Vinaigrette Dressing

½ teaspoon salt
freshly ground black pepper

2 tablespoons wine vinegar
6 tablespoons olive oil

Mix everything together, in a small bowl with a whisk or by shaking the ingredients in a screw-top jar. Chopped green herbs, sugar or honey, dry mustard powder or Dijon mustard, tomato purée or ketchup can be added to vary the flavour.

Mayonnaise

2 egg yolks (or 1 whole egg if using a blender: see below)
1 teaspoon salt
1 teaspoon dry mustard
freshly ground black pepper

200-275 ml (7-10 fl oz) sunflower oil
2-3 teaspoons lemon juice
2-3 teaspoons wine vinegar

MAKES 200-275 ml (7-10 fl oz)

You can make this by hand or use a blender. If you're making it by hand, put the egg yolks into a small bowl with the salt, mustard and pepper and mix well. Then whisk in the oil a drop at a time. When the mixture begins to emulsify you can add a slightly larger amount of oil each time and once it's really thick you can pour the oil in a steady stream, whisking all the time. Lighten the mixture with the lemon juice and add vinegar to taste.

For the blender method, break a whole egg into the goblet and blend quickly with the salt, mustard and pepper. Then add the oil, drop by drop, through the hole in the lid of the blender. When half the oil has been added and you hear the sound of the blender change to a 'glug-glug' noise, you can add the rest in a thin stream. You will probably only be able to use 200 ml (7 fl oz) of the oil using this method. Add lemon juice and vinegar to taste.

White Curd Cheese Dressing

This tastes not unlike mayonnaise for a fraction of the calories.

125 g (4 oz) curd cheese
2 tablespoons natural yoghurt
2 teaspoons olive oil

½ teaspoon wine vinegar
sea salt and freshly ground
    black pepper

Mix everything together to a smooth cream.

Creamy Curried Dressing

2 tablespoons curd cheese or
fromage blanc
2 tablespoons mayonnaise:
home-made or
good quality bought

2 tablespoons natural yoghurt
½-1 teaspoon curry paste
sea salt and freshly ground
black pepper

Put all the ingredients into a small bowl and mix together; adjust the amount of curry paste to taste.

Honey Dressing

This sweet dressing is pleasant on cabbage and root vegetable salads.

1 tablespoon clear honey
1 tablespoon wine vinegar
3 tablespoons sunflower oil

sea salt and freshly ground
black pepper

Mix all the ingredients together.

Tofu Dressing

You need a blender to make this dressing.

150 ml (5 oz) tofu
1 tablespoon olive oil
2 teaspoons wine vinegar
1 clove of garlic, peeled and
  crushed

2 tablespoons chopped chives
sea salt and freshly ground
  black pepper

Put all the ingredients into the blender goblet and blend until smooth.

Spicy Tomato Dressing

2 large tomatoes, skinned
2 tablespoons tomato ketchup
1 teaspoon paprika
2 tablespoons olive oil

1 tablespoon wine vinegar
pinch of chilli powder
sea salt and freshly ground
  black pepper

Put all the ingredients into the blender, blend until smooth, then check seasoning.

Yoghurt and Green Herb Dressing

150 ml (5 fl oz) natural yoghurt
2 teaspoons lemon juice

sea salt and freshly ground
black pepper
2 tablespoons chopped fresh
herbs

Mix all the ingredients together in a bowl; a little crushed garlic can also be added.

Artichoke Heart, Tomato and Watercress Salad

This is one of those salads you can rustle up in a moment; it looks pretty, with the two shades of green, and has a pleasantly piquant flavour. It goes well with pasta dishes and cheese flans.

SERVES 4

1 bunch watercress	1 tablespoon wine vinegar
2 425-g (15 oz) cans artichoke hearts	3 tablespoons olive oil
	freshly ground black pepper
225 g (8 oz) firm tomatoes	sea salt

Wash the watercress, removing the coarse stems; dry in a clean cloth, salad shaker or spinner. Drain the artichoke hearts and slice or quarter them. Put the vinegar into a wooden serving bowl with the oil, a grinding of black pepper and a little salt: not too much, as the artichoke hearts are themselves rather salty. Then put in the artichoke hearts, tomatoes and watercress and turn them over gently to distribute the dressing. Serve immediately.

Avocado and Mushroom Salad

Make sure the avocados are really ripe; they should feel slightly soft when you cradle them in your hand.

SERVES 4

450 g (1 lb) small white button
  mushrooms
2 tablespoons wine vinegar
4 tablespoons olive oil
sea salt and freshly ground
  black pepper

2 avocado pears
2 tablespoons lemon juice
1-2 tablespoons chopped
  fresh chives

Wash mushrooms, pat dry on kitchen paper and slice thinly. Put the slices into a bowl, add the vinegar, olive oil and some salt and pepper, and mix well. Leave on one side for 1 hour. Just before you want to serve the salad, cut the avocado pears in half then twist the two halves in opposite directions to part them and remove the stone. Peel the avocado thinly, cut the flesh into fairly large dice and sprinkle avocado with the lemon juice. Add to the mushrooms, together with the chopped chives, and mix gently.

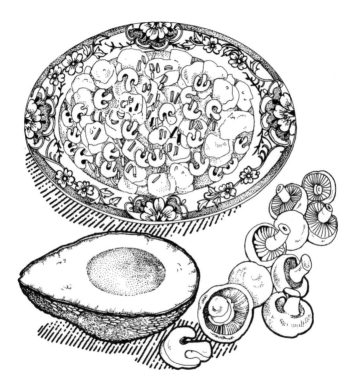

Avocado and Carrot Salad with Raisins and Fresh Ginger Dressing

This is a luxurious salad with a rich creamy dressing and delicious citrus tang of fresh ginger. It can be served as a first course or as a light lunch, with warm wholewheat rolls.

SERVES 4

350 g (12 oz) carrots, scraped and coarsely grated
50 g (2 oz) raisins

4 tablespoons lemon juice
2 ripe avocado pears
sea salt

For the dressing
2 tablespoons mayonnaise
4 tablespoons natural yoghurt
1 teaspoon grated fresh ginger root

a few chopped toasted almonds

Mix together the carrot, raisins and half the lemon juice. Peel and dice the avocado; sprinkle with the remaining lemon juice and add to the carrot. Season and spoon on to a serving dish. Mix together the mayonnaise, yoghurt and ginger, and add seasoning. Spoon over the salad, and sprinkle with toasted almonds.

Banana, Raisin and Peanut Salad

I hit on this idea one day when I wanted to serve curry and rice with extras but didn't have the time or inclination to fiddle around with lots of little bowls of different things. So I put them all in one bowl and this was the result: it's good with curries and other spicy dishes.

SERVES 4

2 bananas
2 tablespoons lemon juice
1 small red pepper, washed, deseeded and chopped
1 bunch spring onions, washed, trimmed and chopped
1-2 tablespoons desiccated coconut

2 tablespoons raisins
4 tablespoons yoghurt or mayonnaise or a mixture
sea salt and freshly ground black pepper
a dash of tabasco
125 g (4 oz) roasted peanuts

Peel and slice the bananas, put into a bowl and sprinkle with lemon juice. Add the chopped red pepper, spring onions, coconut, raisins, yoghurt or mayonnaise and salt, pepper and tabasco. Finally stir in the peanuts and serve at once.

Beetroot with Creamy Horseradish Topping and Walnuts

For this recipe you need cooked beetroot which hasn't been prepared in vinegar: the kind you peel yourself.

SERVES 4

450 g (1 lb) cooked beetroot
1 sweet apple

1 small head of celery

For the dressing
125 g (4 oz) fromage blanc or
   curd cheese
150 ml (5 fl oz) yoghurt or
   soured cream
1 heaped teaspoon horseradish
   sauce

sea salt and freshly ground
   black pepper
25 g (1 oz) fresh walnuts,
   coarsely chopped

Peel the beetroot and cut into medium-sized dice. Dice the apple similarly; wash and slice the celery. Put them into a serving dish. Mix the fromage blanc or curd cheese with the yoghurt or soured cream and the horseradish sauce. Season, then pour this mixture over the beetroot. Sprinkle with the walnuts.

Sweet Cabbage Salad
with Lovage

It's the pungent, aromatic flavour of lovage and the sweet dressing which make this salad different and delicious. If you can grow lovage (and it's easy once you've got it as it comes up every year but needs a good deal of room) try to freeze some for the winter; otherwise use mint or mint sauce concentrate instead. This gives a completely different flavour but is still good!

SERVES 4

1 tablespoon chopped fresh
   lovage or mint, or 1 teaspoon
   mint sauce concentrate
1 tablespoon honey
1 tablespoon wine vinegar

3 tablespoons oil
sea salt and freshly ground
   black pepper
450 g (1 lb) white cabbage,
   coarsely grated

Put the chopped herbs, honey, vinegar, oil and some salt and pepper into a large bowl and mix together to form a dressing. Add the cabbage and mix thoroughly, so that it gets well coated with the sweet herb dressing. Leave for at least 1 hour, so that the cabbage softens a little and absorbs all the flavours.

Cabbage Salad with Red Peppers and Raisins

This salad is excellent with jacket potatoes or a cheese flan.

SERVES 4

3 tablespoons olive oil
1 tablespoon wine vinegar
sea salt and freshly ground
    black pepper
350 g (12 oz) white cabbage,
    washed and shredded
175 g (6 oz) carrot, scraped and
    chopped or coarsely grated

175 g (6 oz) red pepper,
    de-seeded and chopped
2 heaped tablespoons chopped
    parsley, chives or
    spring onions
50 g (2 oz) raisins
50 g (2 oz) roasted peanuts

First make the dressing, straight into the bowl: put the oil and vinegar into the base of a wooden salad bowl, add some salt and pepper and mix. Then put in the cabbage, carrot, red pepper, parsley, chives or spring onions and raisins and turn everything over a few times with a spoon so that they all get covered with the dressing. If possible leave for 1 hour or so: this softens the cabbage and gives the flavours a chance to blend. Stir in the peanuts just before serving.

Carrot, Raisin and Tofu Salad

Tofu or white soya bean curd, which you can now buy from health shops (page 11), makes an interesting addition to a salad mixture and adds protein.

SERVES 4

300 g (10 oz) vacuum pack Morinaga tofu
½-1 teaspoon honey
1 tablespoon soy sauce
1 tablespoon rice vinegar
1 tablespoon sesame oil

350 g (12 oz) carrots, scraped and coarsely grated
1 small green pepper, washed, de-seeded and chopped
50 g (2 oz) raisins
50 g (2 oz) flaked roasted almonds

First, wrap the tofu in several layers of muslin or kitchen paper, place in a sieve with a weight on top and leave for 2 or 3 hours to firm up, then cut into dice.

Put ½ teaspoon honey into a large bowl and stir in the soy sauce, vinegar and sesame oil. Then add the carrots, pepper and raisins and mix well. Gently stir in the tofu. Check the flavouring, adding more honey and salt and pepper if necessary. Sprinkle with the nuts just before serving.

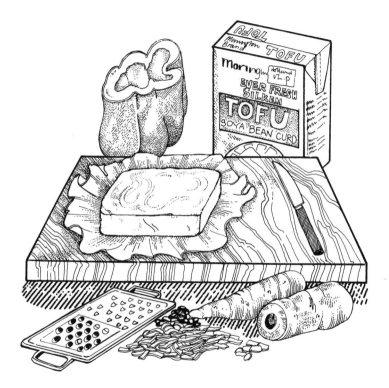

Cauliflower and Apple in Curried Mayonnaise

Serve this salad as a first course or as a light meal, with hot wholewheat cheese scones or crisp warm poppadums.

SERVES 4-6

1 medium-sized cauliflower,
   chopped or coarsely grated
1 carrot, coarsely grated
2 sweet eating apples,
   finely diced

2 tablespoons raisins
1 tablespoon chopped chives
1 tablespoon lemon juice

For the dressing
3 tablespoons natural yoghurt
3 tablespoons mayonnaise
½ teaspoon curry paste

salt and freshly ground pepper
a few crisp lettuce leaves
paprika pepper

Put the cauliflower, carrot and apple into a bowl with the raisins, chives and lemon juice and mix. Combine the yoghurt, mayonnaise and curry paste in a small bowl; season. Put some crisp lettuce leaves on a shallow serving dish and spoon the cauliflower mixture on top. Pour the dressing over the salad, sprinkle with paprika pepper.

Chicory and Walnut Salad

With its crisp, juicy texture chicory makes a delicious salad and is quick and easy to prepare. If you find it rather bitter, try mixing it with a rather sweet dressing. I love the flavour of walnut oil with chicory; it's expensive to buy in this country but only a little gives a wonderful flavour.

SERVES 4

450 g (1 lb) chicory: some red as well as white, if available
2 tablespoons walnut or olive oil
1 tablespoon wine vinegar
sea salt and freshly ground black pepper

25-50 g (1-2 oz) walnuts, roughly chopped
25-50 (1-2 oz) raisins - optional

Wash, trim and slice the chicory leaves. Put the oil, vinegar and some salt and pepper into a salad bowl and mix. Add the chicory, nuts and raisins and turn the salad gently so that everything gets coated with the dressing.

Chicory Flower Salad

This looks like a daisy, with its golden centre and white petals. The centre consists of a creamy cheese dip decorated with carrot rings, and the petals are crisp leaves of chicory stuck around the edge of the dip in two layers. You can eat the salad with your fingers, using the chicory to scoop up the dip.

SERVES 4

225 g (8 oz) curd cheese
125 g (4 oz) finely grated orange-coloured cheese
1 tablespoon tomato ketchup or purée
½ teaspoon paprika pepper
sea salt and freshly ground black pepper

3 heads of chicory, washed and broken into leaves
2 carrots, scraped and cut into rings
juice of 1 lemon
2 tablespoons olive oil

Mix together the curd cheese, grated cheese, tomato ketchup or purée and paprika pepper; season. Heap this mixture up in the centre of a flat serving dish. Stick the chicory all round the edge of this, in two layers, like petals. Toss the carrot slices in lemon juice and arrange over the top of the cheese mixture; spoon the oil over the carrot.

Salad of Chinese Leaves with Beansprouts and a Sweet and Sour Dressing

I have emphasized the Chinese theme by mixing Chinese leaves with crunchy beansprouts and a soy sauce and sesame oil dressing, rather like a salad version of Chinese fried vegetables.

SERVES 4

175 g (6 oz) fresh beansprouts
1 tablespoon clear honey
3 tablespoons sesame oil
2 tablespoons soy sauce
freshly ground black pepper
2.5 cm (1 in) fresh ginger root,
    peeled and finely grated

350 g (12 oz) Chinese cabbage,
    shredded
2 carrots, scraped and coarsely
    grated

Cover the beansprouts with cold water and leave them to soak and crispen while you make the dressing and prepare the other ingredients. Put the honey, oil and soy sauce into the base of a large bowl with a grating of pepper and the ginger, and mix together. Add the Chinese cabbage and carrots, turn them well with a spoon, then drain the beansprouts and add these. Mix well and serve.

Coleslaw

Mayonnaise gives the creamiest, most delicious result in this salad, though for a less calorific version it is also very good made with some natural yoghurt instead of the mayonnaise.

SERVES 4

350 g (12 oz) white cabbage
1 large carrot
1 small onion
50 g (2 oz) sultanas

3 rounded tablespoons
   mayonnaise
sea salt
freshly ground black pepper

Wash and shred the cabbage; scrape and coarsely grate the carrot, peel and finely slice the onion. Put them into a large bowl with the sultanas, mayonnaise and some salt and pepper to taste and mix well. Cover and leave for 2-3 hours before serving if possible: this allows the vegetables to soften and the flavours to blend.

Cucumber and Soured Cream Salad with Fresh Chervil

This creamy, luxurious salad is delicious as a first course with plain light-textured wholewheat bread, or you could serve it as a side salad with fish dishes, in which case you might like to use dill instead of chervil. I like it with hot pasta that's been tossed in a little butter or olive oil and grated Parmesan cheese.

SERVES 4

2 cucumbers
sea salt
150 ml (5 fl oz) soured cream

freshly ground black pepper
1 tablespoon chopped fresh
chervil

Peel the cucumbers, then slice them thinly. Put the slices into a colander, sprinkle with salt, cover with a plate and a weight and leave for at least 30 minutes. Then squeeze the cucumber well and put into a bowl with the soured cream and black pepper to taste. You probably won't need any more salt, but taste and add if necessary. Mix well, then spoon into a serving dish, or individual plates, and sprinkle with the chopped herbs.

Fennel, Carrot and Spring Onion Salad

A refreshing salad that's quick to make, especially if you have an electric grater.

SERVES 4

2 tablespoons lemon juice	225 g (8 oz) carrots, scraped and
2 tablespoons sunflower oil	coarsely grated
salt and freshly ground pepper	4 spring onions, chopped
1 large bulb fennel	

Put the lemon juice and sunflower oil into a large bowl with a little salt and pepper and mix to make a simple dressing. Wash and slice the fennel, trimming off any tough outer layers but keeping any feathery green top: chop these green bits and add to the dressing in the bowl, along with the sliced fennel, grated carrots and spring onions. Mix well. This salad improves with standing: leave for up to 2 hours, turning the ingredients from time to time.

VARIATION

Some raisins and roasted flaked almonds make a pleasant addition.

Fennel and Cucumber Salad

The mixture of fennel and cucumber is refreshing and clean-tasting, and this salad is excellent for when you're in a hurry because it's very simple to make. Good as a side salad with cheese and pasta dishes.

SERVES 4

1 tablespoon wine vinegar
2 tablespoons olive oil
sea salt and freshly ground black
  pepper

1 cucumber
1 large bulb fennel
a little sugar (optional)

Put the vinegar, oil, salt and a grinding of pepper into a salad bowl and mix together. Peel the cucumber and cut into medium-sized dice; wash, trim and slice the fennel, discarding coarse leaves but including any tender feathery leaves. Add the cucumber and fennel to the dressing mixture in the bowl and stir well. Check the seasoning – a touch of sugar can be pleasant in this salad – then serve.

French Bean and Mushroom Salad
with a Coriander Seed Dressing

Here, cooked French beans are marinated, with very lightly cooked button mushrooms, in a spicy dressing of crushed coriander seeds, lemon juice and olive oil. Served with warm wholewheat rolls, this salad makes an excellent starter.

SERVES 4-6

4 tablespoons olive oil
450 g (1 lb) button mushrooms, wiped and halved or quartered
1 small bay leaf
1 tablespoon coriander seed, crushed
juice of 1 small lemon

450 g (1 lb) French beans, cooked and drained
1 tablespoon chopped fresh parsley
sea salt and freshly ground black pepper

Heat the oil in a large saucepan and fry the mushrooms, bay leaf and coriander seeds for 2-3 minutes, until the mushrooms are beginning to soften. Then remove from the heat and cool the mixture quickly by putting it straight into a large bowl and sprinkling with the lemon juice. Add the beans, parsley and some salt and pepper. Leave until completely cold, then chill before serving.

Fruit Salad with Creamy Topping and Toasted Hazel Nuts

Really a main course and a pudding in one, this is a favourite lunch-time salad, especially when served with wholewheat cinnamon and raisin scones straight out of the oven.

SERVES 4

3 ripe dessert apples, diced
2 ripe pears, diced
225 g (8 oz) grapes, halved and de-seeded

2 ripe peaches, stoned and sliced
2 large juicy oranges

For the dressing and topping
225 g (8 oz) curd cheese
4 tablespoons milk

25-50 g (1-2 oz) roasted hazel nuts, crushed

Put the apples, pears, grapes and peaches into a bowl. Then peel the oranges thickly, holding them over the bowl, by first cutting round and round with a sharp knife, then cutting the segments away from the white membranes; add the orange to the bowl. Mix gently and spoon mixture on to a flat serving dish. Combine the curd cheese and milk; pour over the fruit and sprinkle with the nuts.

Green Salad

A classic green salad is refreshing, quick to make and goes with almost any hot dish. You can use any leafy green salad vegetables available and chopped fresh herbs, crushed garlic and sliced onion to taste.

SERVES 4

3 tablespoons olive oil
1 tablespoon wine vinegar
1 clove garlic, peeled and crushed
sea salt and freshly ground
    black pepper
1 lettuce, washed, shaken dry
    and torn into pieces

other salad greens as available:
    watercress, endive, finely
    shredded spinach, dandelion
    or sorrel leaves
2 tablespoons chopped fresh
    herbs: as available
1 mild onion, peeled and sliced
    into thin rings (optional)

Put the oil, vinegar, garlic and seasoning into a salad bowl and mix together. Then just before you want to serve the salad, put all the other ingredients in on top and turn with salad servers until all the leaves are coated with the shiny dressing.

Greek Salad

Guaranteed to evoke instant nostalgia in anyone who has happy memories of Greece, this delicious salad only needs some light-textured bread with it.

SERVES 4

1 cucumber, peeled and cut into chunky dice
450 g (1 lb) firm tomatoes, cut into chunky pieces
1 medium-sized onion, peeled and cut into rings

75-100 g (3-4 oz) black olives
salt and freshly ground pepper
125 g (4 oz) white cabbage, shredded
125 g (4 oz) feta cheese or white Cheshire or Wensleydale

For the dressing
4 tablespoons olive oil

1 tablespoon wine vinegar

Put the cucumber, tomato, onion and olives into a bowl with some salt and pepper and mix. Divide the cabbage between four plates, spreading it out in an even layer, then spoon the cucumber mixture on top and crumble the cheese over that. Combine the oil and vinegar and spoon over the salads just before serving.

Haricot Bean Salad
with Green Herb Dressing

This salad is best made well in advance to allow the flavours time to blend. You can dress the salad while the beans are still hot, leave it to cool, then chill before serving. It makes a good first course or addition to a salad selection; or can be served with hot garlic bread and a green salad or tomato salad.

SERVES 4-6

225 g (8 oz) dried haricot beans, soaked for 2-3 hours, then cooked in water to cover for about 1 hour, until tender
1 teaspoon sugar
½ teaspoon dry mustard powder
1 clove garlic, peeled and crushed

sea salt and freshly ground black pepper
2 tablespoons wine vinegar
6 tablespoons olive oil
2 heaped tablespoons chopped fresh herbs: as available

Drain the beans. Put the sugar, mustard and garlic into a bowl with a little sea salt and a grinding of pepper. Blend to a paste with the vinegar, then gradually stir in the oil to make a dressing. Add the herbs and the beans and mix well. Cool, then chill before serving.

Spicy Lentil Salad
with Fresh Ginger

Serve this salad with the cucumber and soured cream salad on page 34, some chappattis, rolls or poppadums and a tomato side salad.

SERVES 4

4 tablespoons oil
1 large clove garlic, peeled and crushed
1 teaspoon grated fresh ginger root
1 onion, peeled and chopped
225 g (8 oz) small whole brown lentils, from health shops

575 ml (1 pint) water
1 small green or red pepper, de-seeded and finely chopped
1 tablespoon wine vinegar
sea salt and freshly ground black pepper

Heat 2 tablespoons of the oil in a medium-sized saucepan and fry the garlic, ginger and half the onion for 2-3 minutes. Put in the lentils, stir, then add the water. Bring up to the boil, cover and leave to cook slowly until the lentils are tender and all the water is absorbed (about 15-20 minutes). Remove from heat, add remaining oil and onion, the pepper, vinegar and seasoning. Spoon into a serving dish and leave until cool.

Chunky Lettuce Salad with Yoghurt and Herb Dressing

For this salad you need one of those firm-packed lettuces: an Iceberg or Webb's with a very solid heart. It's a quick salad to prepare and makes an excellent side dish with a cooked main course.

SERVES 4

1 Iceberg lettuce or very firm Webb's Wonder	1 tablespoon lemon juice sea salt

For the dressing

1 small clove garlic, peeled and crushed	2 tablespoons chopped fresh herbs: chives, parsley, mint
225 g (10 fl oz) natural yoghurt	freshly ground black pepper

Wash the lettuce as well as you can and remove the outer leaves as necessary. Then cut the lettuce down into thick slices and cut these across, so that you have chunky pieces. Put these on to a flat serving dish, or individual plates, and sprinkle with the lemon juice and some salt. Make the yoghurt dressing by mixing everything together: a quick way to do this is to put all the ingredients into the blender. (If you do this there's no need to chop the herbs first.) Season the sauce, then spoon some over the lettuce chunks and serve the rest separately.

Lettuce Salad with
Sweet Dill Dressing

In contrast to the previous salad, this is a way of adding interest to the soft-leaf varieties of lettuce; it works well in the winter with mediocre lettuces and dried dill weed and is wonderful in the summer with fresh lettuces and dill from the garden.

SERVES 4

1 teaspoon sugar
1 tablespoon fresh dill or
   1 teaspoon dried dill weed
1 tablespoon wine vinegar
2 tablespoons olive oil

sea salt and freshly ground black
   pepper
1 large lettuce, washed and torn
   into pieces
1 small onion, cut into thin rings

Put the sugar, dill, vinegar and oil into a salad bowl with a little salt and pepper and mix well. Add the lettuce and onion, turn the salad gently until all the leaves are coated with the dressing, then serve immediately.

If you want to make this salad ahead of time, prepare the dressing and onion rings and leave on one side; wash and dry the lettuce and put it into a polythene bag in the fridge. The salad can then be assembled in moments just before you want to eat.

Salade Niçoise with Butter Beans

This is a version of Salade Niçoise based on tender cooked butter beans; these absorb the flavours of the olives and dressings well. Serve with warm crusty French bread.

SERVES 4-6

2 tablespoons chopped parsley
1 clove garlic, peeled and crushed
2 tablespoons wine vinegar
6 tablespoons olive oil
salt and freshly ground pepper
125 g (4 oz) butter beans, soaked
   and cooked as described for
   red kidney beans (page 53) or
   1 425-g (15-oz) can

75-100 g (3-4 oz) black olives
450 g (1 lb) French beans, cooked
1 lettuce, washed and shaken dry
450 g (1 lb) tomatoes, sliced

Put the parsley, garlic, vinegar, oil and some salt and pepper into a salad bowl and mix together. Drain butter beans and add, together with the olives, French beans, lettuce and tomatoes. Turn the salad over gently with a spoon until everything is well mixed and glossy with the dressing.

Mexican-style Salad

Serve this salad with warm pitta bread, chappattis or poppadums.

SERVES 4

1 large ripe avocado
2 tablespoons lemon juice
1 clove garlic, peeled and crushed
1 tablespoon olive oil
1 teaspoon wine vinegar
salt and freshly ground pepper
chilli powder
8 large crisp lettuce leaves
125 g (4 oz) red kidney beans,
  soaked and cooked
  (as described on page 53), or
  425 g (15 oz) can, drained

1 small onion, peeled and sliced
  into thin rings
4 firm tomatoes, sliced
1 green pepper, de-seeded and
  thinly sliced
125 g (4 oz) grated cheese or 4
  hardboiled eggs, sliced
a little paprika pepper

Halve, stone, peel and mash avocado; mix with the lemon juice, garlic, oil and vinegar and season with salt, pepper and chilli powder. Lay lettuce leaves on four plates, then layer the beans, onion, tomatoes, green pepper and cheese or eggs on top, ending with a big spoonful of avocado and a sprinkling of paprika.

Onion Side Salad
with Poppy Seeds and Paprika

If you cover onion rings with an oil and vinegar dressing and leave them for an hour or so to marinate they soften and become less hot. This salad is delicious for serving on the side with spicy lentil and rice dishes.

SERVES 4 AS A SIDE DISH

1 tablespoon wine vinegar
2 tablespoons olive oil
sea salt and freshly ground black pepper

2 large mild onions, peeled and sliced into rings
1 tablespoon poppy seeds
2 teaspoons paprika pepper

Put the vinegar and oil into a shallow container with some salt and pepper and mix together. Add the onion rings and mix again, so that they are all covered with the dressing. Sprinkle with the poppy seeds and paprika. Leave on one side for at least an hour, longer if possible: even overnight. Give the salad a stir every so often.

Pasta Salad

Serve this complete-meal salad with grated cheese or a wedge of Brie and some good wholewheat bread.

SERVES 4

175 g (6 oz) wholewheat pasta
   rings
sea salt
1 tablespoon wine vinegar
4 tablespoons olive oil
1 large clove garlic, peeled and
   crushed
freshly ground black pepper

1 ripe avocado
juice of 1 small lemon
125 g (4 oz) firm tomatoes, sliced
125 g (4 oz) firm white button
   mushrooms, wiped and sliced
6 spring onions, washed,
   trimmed and chopped

Cook the pasta in boiling salted water until just tender. Drain well. Mix the vinegar, oil, garlic and some salt and pepper in a large bowl, add the pasta and turn gently with a spoon. Cool, stirring from time to time.

Just before you want to eat the salad, peel and slice the avocado and mix with the lemon juice. Add to the pasta together with remaining ingredients.

51

Red Cabbage Salad with Celery, Apples and Chestnuts

The chestnuts give an unusual touch to this salad which is delicious in the autumn with the first of the red cabbage and celery. Serve it with jacket-baked potatoes split and filled with soured cream, cottage cheese or fromage blanc for a complete meal.

SERVES 4

450 g (1 lb) red cabbage
1 tablespoon wine vinegar
2 tablespoons sunflower oil
sea salt and freshly ground black pepper
2 sweet eating apples, cored and diced

1 celery heart, washed and sliced
125 g (4 oz) cooked chestnuts, halved or quartered
50 g (2 oz) raisins

Wash the cabbage and shred finely or grate coarsely. Put the vinegar and oil into a large bowl with some salt and pepper and stir together. Then add the cabbage, apples, celery, chestnuts and raisins and mix well. This salad can be made an hour or so ahead of time; it keeps well and the cabbage will become softer.

Red Kidney Bean Salad

The secret of making a really good red bean salad is firstly to make it in advance, so that the beans have a chance to soak up the flavour of the dressing, and secondly to include some tomato ketchup in the dressing!

SERVES 4

225 g (8 oz) red kidney beans or 2 425-g (15-oz) cans
2 tablespoons wine vinegar
1 tablespoon tomato ketchup
4 tablespoons olive oil

sea salt and freshly ground black pepper
1 small onion, peeled and cut into thin rings
chopped parsley

Cover beans with cold water and leave to soak overnight; or, for a quick soak, put them into a saucepan, cover with water, boil for 2 minutes, and leave to soak for 1 hour. Then drain and rinse the beans. Put the beans into a saucepan, cover with water and boil vigorously for 10 minutes, then simmer gently for about 1 hour, until beans are tender. Drain. In a large bowl combine vinegar, ketchup, oil and seasoning; add drained beans and onion, and mix well. Cool. Sprinkle with chopped parsley.

Moulded Rice Salad

SERVES 6

225 g (8 oz) long-grain brown rice
575 ml (1 pint) water
sea salt
1 clove garlic, peeled and crushed
1 medium-sized onion, peeled
 and chopped
225 g (8 oz) aubergine, washed
 and cut into small dice

1 small red pepper, de-seeded
 and chopped
2 tablespoons sunflower oil
1 large tomato, skinned and
 chopped
2 drops tabasco sauce
freshly ground black pepper
6 small flat mushrooms, fried

Put rice into a medium-sized saucepan with the water and a
teaspoonful of salt; bring to boil then cover and cook very gently for 45
minutes. Fry the garlic, onion, aubergine and pepper in the oil for 10
minutes; add the tomato and tabasco, cook for 5-10 minutes. Add to
cooked rice and season. Line an 18 cm (7 in) cake tin or soufflé dish
with foil; brush with oil. Put fried mushrooms, black side down, in
base, and spoon rice mixture on top. Press down, chill. Turn out on to
a flat dish and remove foil.

Spinach Salad with Tomatoes, Mushrooms and Leeks

Crisp raw spinach makes a good salad with a very refreshing flavour. Serve this as a side salad; it is especially good with rice and pasta dishes.

SERVES 4

450 g (1 lb) fresh spinach
2 small leeks, washed and
    trimmed
125 g (4 oz) fresh white button
    mushrooms, washed

2 firm tomatoes
1 tablespoon wine vinegar
3 tablespoons olive oil
sea salt and freshly ground black
    pepper

Wash the spinach very well. Dry the spinach in a salad spinner or shaker, then shred it with a sharp knife: I generally include the stalks as well, but you can remove these if you prefer. Slice the leeks finely, discarding the green part; slice the mushrooms, and tomatoes. Put the vinegar and oil into a salad bowl with some salt and pepper; mix well, then add the spinach, mushrooms, tomatoes and leeks and turn them over so that they get coated in the dressing. Serve at once.

Sweetcorn Salad with Spicy Tomato Dressing

With its spicy red dressing, this makes a pleasant side salad and is quick to make.

SERVES 6

450 g (1 lb) fresh or frozen sweetcorn, off the cob

2 spring onions, chopped

For the dressing

2 tablespoons tomato ketchup
1 teaspoon paprika pepper
2 tablespoons olive oil
1 tablespoon wine vinegar

a pinch of chilli powder
2 tomatoes, peeled
sea salt and freshly ground black pepper

Cook the sweetcorn in unsalted boiling water until just tender (2-5 minutes), then drain, mix with the spring onion and leave on one side. Make the dressing by putting all the ingredients into a blender, with some salt and pepper to taste, and liquidizing until fairly smooth. Check seasoning and adjust as necessary. Pour this dressing over the sweetcorn and stir gently so that the sweetcorn all gets covered with it. Put the salad into a clean dish and serve.

Tomato Salad

The important thing here is not to put the dressing on until just before you want to serve the salad or it will become too liquid.

SERVES 4

700 g (1½ lb) firm ripe tomatoes
sea salt and freshly ground black
  pepper
1 tablespoon chopped fresh
  herbs, preferably basil

2 tablespoons olive oil
1 tablespoon wine vinegar

If the tomatoes are really good, veering on the underripe side and very firm, there's no need to peel them unless you specially want to. Otherwise remove the skins by covering the tomatoes with boiling water for 1 minute, then draining and slipping off the skins with a sharp pointed knife. Slice tomatoes, put them into a shallow serving dish and sprinkle them with salt, pepper and the fresh herbs. Just before you want to serve the salad, mix together the oil and vinegar and pour over the top of the salad, turning the tomato gently to distribute the dressing.

Waldorf Salad

Traditionally this salad consists of equal parts of diced celery and apple, bound together in mayonnaise and sprinkled with chopped walnuts. I like to make a lighter version, mixing the mayonnaise with natural yoghurt or soured cream. The salad goes well with cheese dishes and looks good served with some fresh green watercress.

SERVES 4

2 celery hearts, washed and diced
4 large ripe eating apples, diced
3 tablespoons natural yoghurt
3 tablespoons mayonnaise
sea salt

50 g (2 oz) shelled walnuts, roughly chopped
1 bunch watercress, washed and drained
a little paprika pepper (optional)

Put the celery and apple into a bowl and add the yoghurt, mayonnaise and a little salt. Mix well. Spoon the mixture into a serving dish, scatter the walnuts on top and tuck the watercress around the edge. Sprinkle a little paprika on top for an extra touch of colour if liked.

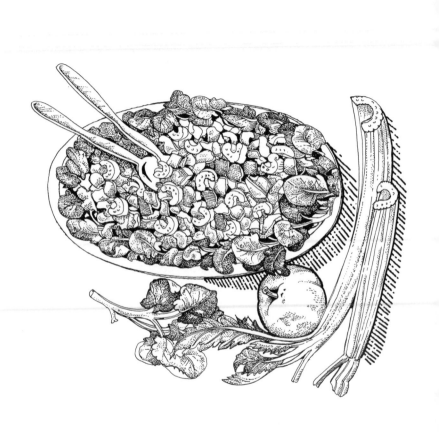

Index

62